JESUS IS

THE BLOOD

THE WORD

AND FAITH

THE ALL ENCOMPASSING NAME OF

JESUS CHRIST

THERE IS NOTHING ELSE YOU NEED

Pamela H Liverett
Vertical Vision Ministries

Revised Edition

JESUS The Blood The Word And Faith

ISBN 978-0-9998887-3-5

Contact information
Email Verticalvision77@aol.com

Cover Art by
http:/www.selfpubbookcovers.com/Kterrier

All scripture given is KJV, WEB, DARBY, ASV
and YLT. All references and meanings from
Strong's Concordance and Thayer's Greek
Lexicon all in public domain.

DEDICATION

My thanks and appreciation to my husband,
George for his support, also to my two-beautiful
daughter in laws Anita for her love, prayers and
support and Rebecca for helping to proof the book
along with my sister Barbara, and Brenda D. for
her continual prayer and support, and many other
people.

Author's Thoughts

Having read through the bible a few times I have
come to the conclusion that we live far below what
we have been given, so now let's take hold of all
that God has given us. The promises of God are
yes and amen. While writing this I heard in my
spirit God saying, "Yes, you can have what I told
you and amen I am faithful, so be it".

JESUS
The Blood The Word
And Faith

The Blood -- OF JESUS

The Word -- OF GOD

And Faith IN BOTH

PAMELA H. LIVERETT

VERTICAL VISION MINISTRIES

I feel as though the scriptures of the Bible have been placed on a plate to serve for a setting in our lives. The explanation of experiences and life stages presents excellent examples of how true God's word is! Pam demonstrates if we simply believe as a child and would believe on God's promises, and know and abide by His word, those promises are implemented by God. I go from the first page to the last and can read His word out loud and I know He hears me. I must believe, trust and place His word in my heart because His word never fails us. Thank you, Pam, for your extensive research that rekindles your spiritual fire of God's promises.

Kelley Wolfe Browning

****

Going through the book I have found it to be word based and I like that about it. You touch on faith, authority, our words, our thoughts, our God given right and inheritance as His children. I found it to be a great resource for praying for the miraculous in our lives. You did a great job. Thank you for giving the book to us.

Amanda Laird

****

Upon receiving a copy of your book.
"Jesus The Blood The Word And Faith" I was
overjoyed. The book is based upon the Holy
Scripture and as a believer I hold the scripture
dear. Your book really brought those scripture out
and made them clear and showed me how to use
the word better and why. There were times that as
I read, the Holy Spirit would rise up within me and
I just wanted to leap and shout, then at other times
I would weep due to the word being confirmed to
my spirit. It was a book for the hour because at
this time I was sick, and I was believing God for
my healing. I found this book a blessing and a
word of assurance for me. I know the scripture
used are true and from the bible, the examples you
used tell me that you are a person that I know you
to be, you are steadfast and a strong believer in
God's word. You and I have sat and talked in
church and shared our feelings about the scripture.
You are strongly knowledgeable in the word,
which to me make this book important and very
useful to anyone who will accept what it says.
Thank you so much your friend and brother in
Christ.

Stephen Winters.

****

Thank you, Pamela Liverett, for your dedication and diligence toward providing this most profound book. Through your God given writing abilities you convey to the reader an awareness of the gift of healing. If you desire healing for your mind, body, soul or spirit, this resourceful book is the one for you. Within its pages you will find the powerful word of God available and ready for covering your every need. Allow this book to take you on a healing journey. Your faith will be strengthened, your hope renewed, and your health restored. Greater knowledge and understanding will unfold as you receive and insight that healing is not only possible but also available and accessible. I can personally recommend this book. "Jesus The Blood The Word And Faith." Scripture is provided for declaring healing for yourself, your family, and others. Everything you need toward discovering the answer to your healing questions can be found in this book.

I urge you to get a copy.

Brenda Dodd

****

In this century information fly's at us from every direction. Occasionally a grain of truth comes our way but now we must know the integrity of the source of the facts in order to accept them as truth. This beautifully written book states truth in a simple way and gives its place in The Scripture, the ultimate source of Truth. An inspired work aimed at the people caught up in the world and blind to the Truth in God's word. It will become a permanent part of my reference books.

Tamera A. Thomas

****

THE VISION

Back in 2004, I had a vision while driving to work. I was praying for someone when suddenly I was in heaven. I saw Jesus sitting on a rock looking at me with His head tilted, when suddenly this shockwave reverberated throughout heaven. The power of the shockwave was felt on my body like a hurricane wind. The vibrations of this shockwave went across the great expanse of heaven, the whole of heaven felt and knew what this power was, and I instantly knew someone had said the name JESUS. At that moment I realized how powerful the name of Jesus is when we speak His name.

I always remember my mother telling me during the blitz in England that when a bomb went off it sent shockwaves through the air and killed many people.

Don't you know the devils are afraid of that name and don't want you to know just how powerful it becomes when you say, "IN THE NAME OF JESUS."

Philippians 2:9 Wherefore God also hath highly exalted Him, and given Him a NAME which is above every name.

Colossians 1:16 For by Him were all things created, that are in heaven, and that are on earth, visible and invisible, whether they be thrones, or dominions, principalities, or powers: all things were created by Him and for Him.

This man that created all that was created, gave us that power to fight against the wiles of the devil.

Ephesians 6:11 Put on the whole armour of God, that you may be able to stand against the wiles of devil.

Seriously what more do we need!!!!!!

Whenever the name of JESUS is spoken here on earth it creates a shockwave, the same power that is in heaven, that power ripples through the earths atmosphere even though we don't see it, that's how and why we can proclaim healing, salvation, deliverance, peace, joy, and so much more just by saying **"In The Name Of Jesus"** Wow, Wow, Wow. How awesome is that.

That means living a victories life is possible no matter the circumstances, because He is ever mindful of our situation and our names are written in the palm of His hand.   Isaiah 49:16

THE BLOOD

Have you ever wondered why God chose blood for the atonement of sin, like the animal sacrifices of a pure unblemished lamb in the old testament?

What made Jesus blood superior to human blood when conceived in His mother's womb? While pondering this, I discovered that the blood that flows through the unborn child does not come from the mother, but at the moment of conception it is the father that gives this life-giving substance to the fetus. This then enables the unborn child to produce its own blood in the womb, the mothers blood and the baby's blood never co-mingle or cross over.

Luke 1:35 The angel answered her, "The Holy Spirit will come on you, and the power of the Most High will overshadow you. Therefore also the

*Holy One which is born from you will be
called the Son of God"*

When Jesus was conceived in the Virgin Mary, it was the Holy Ghost that over shadowed her, and Divine Heavenly blood was imparted to this unborn child. This explains why the blood of Jesus is so Pure, so Holy, so different, and so Powerful; more than any other blood of human or animal. This Holy blood had to be in a fleshly body, but all humanity was conceived in sin from the garden. King David said in,

*Psalms 51:5 Behold, I was brought
forth in iniquity. In sin my mother
conceived me.*

There needed to be a sinless body to hold this precious life-giving, lifesaving blood. Jesus was the incarnate word of God complete with this heavenly blood that was to be shed for all mankind for the remission of sin. When Jesus came to earth He also gave us the power and authority in His name. Wow!

THE POWER OF THE BLOOD

In Exodus 12 the Passover was instituted through God by the shedding of innocent blood from a lamb without blemish.

Exodus 12:13 And the blood shall be to you for a token upon the houses where you are, and when I see the blood, I will pass over you, and the plague shall not be upon you to destroy you, when I smite the land of Egypt.

Exodus 12:23 For the Lord will pass through to smite the Egyptians; and when He sees the blood on the lintel, and the two side posts, the Lord will pass over the door, and will not suffer the destroyer to come in unto your houses to SMITE YOU. Emphasis added.

God told Moses to speak to all the congregation of Israel saying, "put the blood on the door posts and lintels". God didn't say He would do it. He told the Israelites to apply the blood and the people had to be proactive and do it by faith, trusting that it would work, but if anyone did not put the blood on the door posts and lintels the death angel would not be stopped from entering in. I repeat, the people had to be proactive and apply the blood.

This was a foreshadowing of what Jesus was going to do for us. He was beaten and nailed to the cross. His blood dripped and poured to the earth for our healing, our salvation, our protection, and so much more. We can, symbolically follow that pattern in prayer, and apply the blood of Jesus Christ to ourselves, our families, friends, peoples and nations, when we say,

"Father God in Jesus name, I plead the blood and apply the blood of Jesus Christ over my family, (list names) friends, Israel, Jerusalem the Israelis and to protect Christians around the world and those you want saved, from all sickness, harm and danger, accidents and incidents of all kinds, and against any and all wickedness that would come against us, Protect us from natural disasters, man-made disasters and protect us from your judgement that we deserve as a people, because of our passiveness we have allowed sin to reign in our nations, forgive us Lord. I ask for your wisdom in all these things Father God, in Jesus mighty powerful name, Thank you Jesus."

I have done this for many years and it works. Several years ago, I was driving to work when about 20 minutes into my drive I suddenly became aware of seeing several dark blue trucks. My oldest son had a dark blue truck, so I knew God was telling me to pray for him, so I did praying the blood of Jesus over him to protect him. That evening I found out he had got his arm caught between two large cast iron pipes on a conveyor belt, but he was able to pull his arm free before it ripped his arm off or killed him. He only had a few scrapes and bruises on that arm. Praise God for the blood. You cannot convince me that pleading and applying the blood of Jesus Christ in prayer over him did not protect him, because I know it did. I believe God sometimes gives us warning of things the devil has planned for us, so God will give us a little nudge to pray about a situation, but sometimes we are dull of hearing like I was, it took me 20 minutes to realize God was trying to get my attention.

I call it **Proactive Prayers** when we pray to prevent anything from happening instead of praying after something has already happened.

The blood of Jesus is very powerful as Isaiah 53 tells us it covers all we have need of.

Isaiah 53:5 But He was wounded for our transgressions, He was bruised for our iniquities: the chastisement of our peace was upon Him; and with His stripes we are healed.

But how can we get to where that becomes second nature in us to pray? **It is through Worship, reading His Word, communing with Him in our own home our secret place. What I call loving on Him for who He is and not for what He can do for me; to seek His face not His hand. We love our children unconditionally not expecting anything in return but just to love us back, that's all. So, it is with God He wants us, nothing more, nothing less just us. How awesome is that!**

SEEING IS BELIEVING
NO
BELIEVING IS SEEING

Hebrews 11:1 Now faith is the substance of things hoped for the evidence of thing not seen.

Hebrews 11:1 Is a very familiar verse so I want to give a little insight into how this amazing scripture can have a greater impact on how we live our life in today's world.

Breaking it down it would read:

Immediately and instantly I know I have the assurance and the confidence of what I have expected, is already an accomplished fact. I have proof and certainty of that which has been done, even though in the natural it absolutely cannot be seen yet, I will behold and see it.

Faith is seeing what God sees - God sees life, wholeness, peace, joy, happiness. God does not see despair, sickness, misery, tears, and pain as outcome for us.

FAITH CHANGES YOUR OPTIONS OF THE CIRCUMSTANCES

We need to believe in the tangible substance of the things we desire so we can see them in the spirit. We must set the vision before us being the oracle of God, the command, revelation and authoritative declaration that:

Exodus 23:25 And you shall serve the Lord your God, and He shall bless your bread, and your water; and I will take sickness away from the midst of you.

Already done. How much clearer of a command do we need?

Most of us will believe if we see it first. For example, like the show me state, but God doesn't work on those terms. He says believe first then I'll show you. That's called FAITH. When you read and discern the word of God rightly dividing the word of truth, the spirit man inside you begins to see through the eyes of God and you understand and see by the spirit that believing first is really seeing. You believe what the word says. Like a child we must take God at His word and if He said it, then it must be true. If people really believed God's word they would stand firm on that word, but if a doctor has a new treatment they will have faith in that treatment and the doctor, over God. WHY? Because they can see the doctor face to face, ask questions, and see the treatment. But with God you trust and believe His word without seeing any manifestation of hope and healing but see the healing through the eyes of faith until it has manifested. Faith requires you to believe in something and someone you cannot see.

Matthew 17:20 And Jesus said unto them, Because of your unbelief: for verily I say unto you, If ye have faith as a grain of mustard seed, ye shall say unto this mountain, Remove hence to yonder place; and it shall remove; and nothing shall be impossible for you.

Do we have Hebrews 11:1 **A Now Faith?**

Do we really believe what God says, or is it only surface belief? My little ones, like any child, they believe what you say you will do. No if, ands or buts about it, and if you do not do what you said you would do, oh boy they grill you. "You said you would. Why did you not do it? You said you would." Over and over again until you wished you had followed through and done what you said. They want to know why you did not keep your word. Do we believe God like that, expectantly with pure trust and belief in His word?

IT IS A MINDSET

So, to be healed the way God intended is a mindset.
A - Mind - Set - On - God.

Do we really, really believe that?

A mindset means I have decided on something - I am focused. In fact, laser focused on something. I am bound and determined. My thought process is, I have decided; no if, ands, or, buts about it. It's almost stubborn like. To have our minds set on God's word means we must know His word and know Him. If you don't know someone very well it's hard to take seriously what they say about a situation, but if you know them really well you believe them without doubting, so it is with God and His word.

So, what is a mindset? The answer to that question also depends on what type of Christian we are; a surface Christian, apart-time Christian, a slack Christian, or one that loves God with all their being and runs after Him every moment. The first three have only head knowledge of God and His truths. The word of God that they read only resides in the head, the soul part of mankind. The Christian seeking God daily, worshiping Him, loving on Him, not asking for things but seeking His face not His hand, he has a channel opened up from his head/soul that goes down into his spirit man. So, when he reads Gods word it flows deep inside of him and resonates throughout his being. It gets embedded deep down in his spirit, so he knows, that he knows beyond the shadow of a doubt the truth and realness of God's word to him and the world. The difference is the type of relationship each have with their Heavenly Father. Let me explain it this way.

As a mother I gave birth to my children, and I wanted to spend lots of time with them, I wanted them to spend time with me, and I was interested in everything they did. As their mom I wanted to know about everything that concerned them, and I wanted to be a part of their lives every day. I didn't just see them once a week and touch base with them like asking how are you doing this week? then forget them for another week or so. No! I communed with them every day, I loved them every day all day long.

If we had that kind of thinking mentality with our Heavenly Father we would know Him, believe and trust His word to us, and have an unshakable faith that He is true to His word and He cannot lie to us.

Numbers 23:19 God is not a man, that He should lie; neither a son of man, that He should repent; hath He said, and shall He not do it? Or hath He spoken, and shall He not make it good.

He won't lie to us, I know, that I know, that I know, needs to vibrate through our entire being.

> *2 Corinthians 10:5 Casting down imaginations, and every high thing that exalts itself against the knowledge of God and bringing into captivity every thought to the obedience of Christ.*

THE WORD

So now the next point, how did God intend to heal us.

> *Psalms 107:20 He sent His **WORD** and healed them and delivered them from their destructions.* Emphasis added

Well, who became the word and was made manifest in human form to give us life in the fullest form? **JESUS.**

God expects us to take Him at His **word** like our children do us. We have to have our minds set on this one thing, if God said it I must believe, it's child-like faith. Do we really, really believe like that. If we are not sure or have doubt about what God says to us, then we can't be sure of what He will do for us in any situation whether healing, finances, peace, joy, comfort, deliverance etc, etc, etc. His living word has to resonate through our being, so that we have an unshakeable knowing that Jesus gave us His authority.

This is the Great Commission in

> *Mark 16:15-20 "Go ye into all the world and preach the gospel to every creature. 16. He that believeth and is baptized shall be saved; but he that believeth not shall be damned. 17. And these signs shall follow them that believe;* **in My name shall they cast out devils; they shall speak with new tongues. 18. They shall take up serpents; and if they drink any deadly thing, it shall not hurt them; they shall lay hands on the sick and they shall recover.** *19. So then after the Lord had spoken unto them, He was received up into heaven, and sat on the right hand of God. 20. And they went forth, and preached everywhere, the Lord working with them, and confirming the word with signs following.* Amen Emphasis added

Them that believe are those that receive Christ as their personal Savior. They can cast out devils, speak with new tongues. If they drink any deadly thing it shall not hurt them. Lay hands on the sick and they SHALL recover. Not, maybe recover, but shall/will recover.

Now we have to decide did Jesus really mean for us to do this, then why do so few have signs following them? Jesus was not being arbitrary, Yes indeed, Jesus meant what He said. It is the Spirit of the Living God that resides in us to continue to do the work that Jesus tells and commands us to do. To go into all the world and preach the gospel, the glad tidings of salvation through Christ and then signs will follow. The signs show the unbeliever the truth about the grace and mercy of God, to heal the spirit, soul and body.

AUTHORITY

Matthew 10.1 And when he had called unto Him his twelve disciples, He gave them power against unclean spirits, to cast them out, and to heal all manner of sickness and all manner of disease.

Mark 6:7 And He called unto him the twelve and began to send them forth by two and two; and gave them power over unclean spirits.

Luke 9:1 Jesus called His disciples and gave them power and Authority over all devils and to cure diseases. 2. He sent them out to preach the kingdom of God and to heal the sick.

We were given the right to cancel the assignment of things the devil sends our way, through the blood of Jesus Christ and His Name.

Exodus 15:26 And said, if thou wilt diligently hearken to the voice of the LORD thy God and will do that which is right in His sight and will give ear to His commandments, and keep all His statutes, I WILL PUT NONE OF THESE DISEASES upon you, which I have brought upon the Egyptians; for I am the Lord that HEALETH YOU.
Emphasis added

How did you lose your authority, and why do we serve God if the same things happen to us as non-Christians in the world,???? We receive same

28

sickness, same problems. Why would anyone want to serve God if Christians have same problems as them? We indeed are most miserable if all we have to look forward to is heaven as an escape, from gloom and doom while we wait to get there. We handle it the same way as non-Christians, but we are supposed to be above our problems not eye level with them. What we have inside us makes us handle things differently with a different attitude. Jesus came so we would reign here on earth with His power and authority to set people free from bondage and sin and to give them life and life more abundantly through His name.

> *1 John 5:4-5 For whatsoever is born of God, overcomes the world, and this is the victory that overcomes the world even our faith. 5 Who is he that overcomes the world, but he that believes that Jesus is the son of God.*

Nowhere in the bible did Jesus leave someone sick. He healed everyone that wanted to be healed. The only exception to that was in His home town where they could not believe that one of their own could have such wisdom and they were offended.

Matthew 13:58 And He did not many mighty works there because of their unbelief.

That should tell us that we have a right not to be sick. If Christ is in us and we abide in Him and He abides in us we become one.

1 John 2:27 But the anointing which you have received of Him abides in you, and you need not that any man teach you: but as the same anointing teaches you of all things, and is truth, and is no lie, and even as it has taught you, you shall abide in Him.

John 15:4 Abide in me, and I in you. As the branch cannot bear fruit of itself, except it abide in the vine; no more can you, except you abide in me.

John 15.7 If you abide in me, and my words abide in you, you shall ask what you will, and it shall be done unto you.

What more do you need!!!

Abide = G3306 and Thayer's Greek lexicon, A given place, state, relation, to not depart or leave, to continually be present, unbroken fellowship, dwell, to remain, tarry.

Words = G4487 Rhema the living words spoken by Jesus, the living word that was the same as the spoken word when "God said", and everything came into existence with His spoken living word.

Whether you like it or not He created us as speaking spirits, we are created in His image and likeness to do the things that Jesus did. He said we would do greater things. So how would we do that? By speaking of and to those things that are not as though they are.

Romans 4:17 (As it is written, I have made thee a father of many nation,) before him who he believed, even God, quickeneth the dead, and calleth those things which be NOT as though there WERE. Emphasis added.

Genesis 1:3 God said, "Let there be Light" and there was light.
God said, *HE* SPOKE. Emphasis added.

*John 5:38 And you have not His word
abiding in you: for whom He hath sent,
Him you believe not.*

*John 6:63 It is the spirit that quickens;
the flesh profits nothing: the words that I
speak to you, they are spirit, and they are
LIFE. Emphasis added*

If God said it then believe it, no matter how
outrageous it may seem.

So, if we believe that Jesus Christ is the son of
God then we can overcome the world and not have
any part of the sickness that has fallen on the earth.
If we fully understand the depth of God's word to
us, and get it moved from head knowledge to heart
knowledge, and into our spirit man.

You do not let a robber into your house, why let
a thief and robber into your body. It is easier to stop
sickness from entering into your body than trying to
get it out after it has moved in. It's harder to get
renters or squatters out of your house or building
once they have moved in. It is easier to keep the
house secure locked up and protected to stop them
from entering. "Prevention is better than cure".

It is easier to stop something before it starts than to try to fix it after it has gotten hold of you. Just like a drug addiction or alcohol it is better not to start taking drugs or drinking or anything else that will take over and control you. It is the same with sickness. Refuse it entry into your body with the word of God and use the authority Jesus gave us to stop it from entering into us. It is a Mindset. Let sin in, it will take hold and will bring forth death. There is an old saying my mother used to say to me, "I give you an inch, you take a yard". You give sickness a little opening by entertaining the thought of it; I guarantee it will barge in with vengeance.

KEYS

Again, to break this down so we can understand what Jesus meant. Jesus talking to Peter, who represents the church, said in,

Matthew 16:19 And I will give unto thee the keys of the kingdom of heaven and whatsoever thou shalt bind on earth shall be bound in heaven: and whatsoever thou shalt loose on earth shall be loosed in heaven.

What is bound in heaven can be bound on earth.

To bind is to tie up, hold fast with ropes or chains so it cannot get loose. What is contrary to God's word, death, sickness, fear, hopelessness, mental instability, unhappiness, loss of joy, loss of peace, poverty, demonic attacks, and many more such things. Do we use the word Jesus gave us to bind sickness and problems?

What is loosed in heaven can be loosed on the earth, so we can untie and set free, what is allowed in heaven; joy, peace, love, sound mind, deliverance, healing, safety, prosperity, life, hope, happiness, joy full of glory, overwhelming love, protector, a shield round about us, angels guarding us, and so much more.

A key gives access to someone. Depending if the key is loaned or given, will determine the usage example, renting a house for a period of time will give you full access to use all it pertains to, but cannot change anything without permission. A key to my own house gives me full access to do what I want, change, tear down, or build. I have total control of the entire house.

The keeper of the keys has the legal power and authority to open and shut the door, - the

keys being the understanding of binding and loosing what to bind and what to lose, as we have been given that authority. We are the surrogate of this authority that Jesus gave us here on earth.

The one who holds the keys has the power and authority to open and shut the door. Jesus gave us His keys of authority.

The keys of the Kingdom of God are whatever you're in need of, God has provided.

<u>Jesus...... you are the key to life, the doorway to health, peace, joy, and happiness. You brought the kingdom of God down to us. All of God's goodness which is everything good that is in heaven, you brought to us if we will take and receive it.   Thank you, JESUS.</u>

> *Hebrews 11:3 Through faith we understand that the worlds were framed by the word of God so that things which are seen were not made of things which do appear.*

In other words, things which are seen were made with things we cannot see.

In God's world what you don't see is what you get. God is spirit, we are carnal and fleshly. Things in this realm are temporal. so, the idea is to keep our eyes focused on God, So we can perceive with our spiritual eyes spiritual insight for what God has for us, according to His word. Even though His word is very clear on what He has given us. **Jesus gave us His authority and the keys to death hell and the grave, but they are still lying on the floor. Very few of us have bothered to pick them up, and some that have picked them up don't know how to use them.**

ABUNDANTLY

Being sick is not having life more abundantly.

John 10:10 The thief comes to steal, kill, and destroy, I have come that they might have life, and that they might have it more ABUNDANTLY. Emphasis added

This is a truly and amazing scripture if we could just get a hold of the true meaning of what Jesus is saying in John 10:10.

Jesus came to bring us real **LIFE**, I love the

Blue Letter Bible they list in Strong's Concordance G2222 that life means, real genuine life, a life active and vigorous, devoted to God., blessed in this world all those who put their trust in Christ. The absolute fullness of life and the state of one who is possessed of vitality and animate, which is having life. This is the life He brought.

Now see what happens when He gives us life and **Life** more **Abundantly**, according to Strong's Concordance G4053 and Thayer's Greek Lexicon, we are supposed to have abundant life over and above, more than necessary, superadded, exceeding abundantly, supremely, something more than we have, more much more than all, superior, extraordinary, surpassing, uncommon, superiority, more eminent (to stand out above others), exceeding some measure, super abundant, abound, superior in quality.

WOW!!! Doesn't sound like we as Christians should be walking around with cancer, heart condition, diabetes, arthritis, high cholesterol, or any other ailment. Somehow, we have not taken God at His word, but instead we have taken the word of the world which says if your family had this or that, you will have it to. If you're around certain sicknesses, you will catch it too.

The world view says old and sickness goes hand in hand. I say……..NADA NOWAY! I am just passing through and I am not picking up any sick luggage on my way through. My mind is set on God and what His word says. God didn't say we had to succumb to this world's sickness. He delivered us from bondage and sin to give us salvation and life more abundantly through His name, His death on the cross and His resurrection. Why else did He come? Amen, Thank You Jesus end of story.

As a side note read Joshua 14:7-12. Joshua and Caleb were the two spies that came back and told Moses we can take this land and 45 years later Caleb speaking to Joshua says;

> *Joshua 14:10-12 And now behold, the Lord hath kept me alive, as he said these forty and five years, even since the Lord spake this word unto Moses, while the children of Israel wandered in the wilderness and now lo I am this day fourscore and five years old. 11: As yet I am as strong this day as I was in the day that Moses sent me: as my strength was then, even so is my strength now, for war both to go out and to come in. 12.*

Now therefore give me this mountain,
whereof the Lord spake in that day.

Caleb is 85 years old and wants to take the land he was promised. As you think, so you will be.

God is not a respecter of persons. What He will do for one He will do for another.

Acts 10:34 Then Peter opened his mouth and said of a truth I perceive that God in no respecter of persons.

1 John 5:4,5 For whatever is born of God overcomes the world. This is the victory that has overcome the world; your FAITH. 5. Who is he who overcomes the world, but he who believes that Jesus Christ is the Son of God. Emphasis added

THE THREE R'S

RESIST - REBUKE - REFUSE

We know that sickness, poverty, etc. is not from God. I use this analogy; you use an umbrella to keep you dry and protected from the rain, so spiritually if you come out of the umbrella of Gods protection then the devil can attack you. Stay in the presence of God with prayer, reading, and worship daily, then at the first inkling of something **resist it, rebuke it, and refuse it.** And say "I do not want it, I won't have it, I'm not having it" etc. I refuse it in Jesus Name and I am healed and whole by the power of the blood of Jesus Christ. Amen, Amen, Amen.

I have prayed this for many years whenever I came close to anyone who was sick I would say this simple prayer and I never thought anymore about it, but I never did catch what they had. But then one time I did not say this prayer, it was several years ago when my husband was coughing, sneezing and felt really bad with a cold and for the first time in many years I did not say my little prayer and guess what, I got very sick with the same cold that he had. That taught me a very valuable lesson: We do have more power in what we speak in pray than we realize.

*James 4:7 Submit yourselves therefore to God. **Resist the devil, and he will flee from you.*** Emphasis added

Having done everything we know we can do we need to stand firm that no matter what happens or what thoughts come to our mind, we will not change our mind and we will stay focused on what God says about the situation. By staying focused the devil will bolt.

Ephesians 6:13 Wherefore take unto you the whole armour of God, that ye may be able to withstand in the evil day, and having done all, to stand. 14. Stand therefore, having your loins girt about with truth, and having on the breastplate of righteousness: 15. And your feet shod with the preparations of the gospel of peace, 16. Above all, taking the shield of faith, where with ye shall be able to quench all the fiery darts of the wicked. 17. And take the helmet of salvation, and the sword of the Spirit, which is the word of God; 18. Praying always with all prayer and supplication in the Spirit and watching thereunto with all perseverance and supplication for all saints.

THE TONGUE – OUR TONGUE

Proverbs 18:21 Death and life are in the power if the tongue: **and they that love it shall eat the fruit thereof.**
Emphasis added

Our words often get us in trouble when we invite sickness into us by claiming ownership such as; my diabetes, my cancer, my heart disease, my nerves are bad, my depression, my, my, my. It doesn't belong to you, but you have just spoken death over yourself or someone else. God says to speak life not death. It's a state of mind you have what you speak. Read it again **"they that love it shall eat the fruit thereof" so if you speak death you have eaten the fruit of death, then speak life and you will eat the fruit of life.**

Several years ago I speaking to someone about what a doctor had told them, I said you need to pray and refuse that sickness, they looked at me and said quote "the doctor said I had this and he knows what he's talking about" Instantly I felt something happen in the spirit around them. They had just come into agreement in the negative, and today still have this issue.

Do not give sickness a way in. Do not open the door in agreement, do not let it in. Put your foot on its neck and say, "I refuse you coming into my body or my family, I don't want it! I won't have it! I'm not having it or receiving it! It is not gonna happen in Jesus Name. Be adamant, passionate, forceful, knowing you have God's word to back you up.

> *1 John 4:4 Greater is He that is in you, than he that is in the world.*

Do not communicate with sickness or talk to it by pondering on it. You do not have to accept what your body is telling you. Who rules you? Spirit, Soul or Body. We are not of this world, so we should not be ruled by this world or the body/soul.

> *John 15:16,19 You have not chosen me, but I have chosen you, and ordained you, that you should go and bring forth fruit, and that your fruit should remain: that whatsoever you shall ask the Father in my name, he may give it you. 19. If you were of this world the world would love his own: but because you are NOT of this world, but I have chosen you OUT of the world, therefore the world hates you.*

Jesus praying to His father says;

John 17:14 I have given them thy word, and the world hated them, because they are NOT of the world, even as I am NOT of the world. Emphasis added

2 Corinthians 1:20 For the promises of God in Him are yea and in Him amen, unto the Glory of God by us.

Many Christians allow things to come on them.

Hosea 4:1 Hear the word of the Lord, ye children of Israel: for the Lord hath a controversy with the inhabitants of the land, because there is no truth, nor mercy, nor knowledge of God in the land.

Hosea 4:6. My people are destroyed for lack of knowledge.

What knowledge is He talking about, in Hosea 4:1 God says hear the word of the Lord, and ends with there is no truth, no mercy and no knowledge of God in the land. In other words they had no divine instruction. The religious leaders gave no knowledge and instruction about their God. They did not know God.

THROW AWAY THE MOLD, AND THINK OUTSIDE YOU THOUGHTS

The control is in the place between your ears, your mind. It all comes down to what you do with your thoughts, and how you think. It's a mind game in essence so do not ponder on anything negative etc. For example, when fasting, if you ponder, or get your mind on food, this will weaken your resolve and faith to fast that day. Same thing with your body. The first moment you feel an ache or pain in your body don't think about it like I'm getting a cold, or having pains in other parts of the body. Instantly refuse it and cast it off in Jesus Name. Don't ponder and think about it because when you do, you have opened the door to let it in and it will be harder to get it off you. We need healing the way God intended. It is a mindset if we only had God we would go to God first and not the doctor first and then pray. We have got to take our negative thoughts captive and cancel them in the name of Jesus and proclaim the promises of God.

2 Corinthians 10:5 Casting down imaginations, and every high thing that exalts itself against the knowledge of God and bringing into captivity every thought to the obedience of Christ.

Again, at the first inkling of something **resist it, rebuke it, refuse it,** don't want it, not having it. Stand firm on this and the devil will flee.

Hebrews 11:1 Now faith is the substance of things hoped for, the evidence of things not seen.

Of course, I know God uses doctors, I am not saying never go to the doctor, it was God who gave them the knowledge. As Christians our focus should always be God first. I am talking about faith in God.

I know there will be some people that will say what I'm suggesting is wrong, but again that is the world's mindset. I'm stating what the word of God says we have by using the authority of the name of Jesus.

GOD GIVEN RIGHT

People are not willing to fight for their healing and refuse it in Jesus Name, or do not know that they can refuse it, so they are more willing to accept the sickness. Why? They don't really know their God, His word and His provision for them. You know what your spouse, kids, other family member, and friends will do for you, because you know them well, but we do not know God or His word that well or well enough.

> *2 Corinthians 1:20 For however many are the promises of God, in him is the "Yes." Therefore, also through him is the "Amen", to the glory of God through us.*

> *3 John 1: 2 Beloved, I pray that you may prosper in all things and be healthy, even as your soul prospers.*

Again, I am not saying don't go to the doctor, I am saying learn and understand what God says. By all means go to the doctor if you need to but pray first and pray as you go. The trouble is when we feel something like a cold, sinus or upset stomach etc., we forget to pray and cancel it right then but run to the medicine cabinet when in fact if you need to run to the medicine cabinet you should continue praying resisting, rebuking and refusing you will find that the issue goes away much faster than ever before which in turn builds your faith.

Also remember God gave us natural remedies and products for our health and healing as needed.

But we come into agreement with what our body says and not what the word says about us. We come into agreement with our body in the negative. Stop letting the body dictate to your spirit and soul.

Jesus came so we would reign here on earth with His power and authority to set people free from bondage, to give them life and life more abundantly through His name.

PILGRIMS

Hebrews 11:13 Those all died in faith, not having received the promises, but having seen them afar off, and were persuaded of them, and embraced them, and   confessed that they were strangers and pilgrims on the earth.

*1 Peter 2:11 Dearly beloved, I beseech
you as strangers and pilgrims, abstain
from fleshly lusts, which war against the
soul.*

A pilgrim is someone who is passing through a place they are not homesteading or making it a permanent residence.

Why have Christians allowed things to come on them? They have decided to homestead this world and decided to just settle in down here. This should not be, we are pilgrims passing through.

*1 Peter 2:9 But you are a chosen
generation, a royal priesthood, an holy
nation a peculiar people; that you
should show forth the praises of Him
who hath called you out of darkness into
His marvelous light.*

If we are passing through this world then we are not partakers. When you pass through another country you do not pick up their culture or take part and share, and say this is what or who I am. So why do we pick things from this world and say this is me. Such as my parents and my grandparents had this problem, so I will have it too. **No! No! No!** That's a worldly mindset and these are generational curses as in sicknesses drug and alcohol problems divorce abusive behavior and other family issues and traits. These can be cancelled by the blood of Jesus Christ. **Trait means inherited characteristic**

If we are in an environment where there is a contagious disease, or when we are around someone that has a contagious disease or virus, like the flu, coughing, sneezing, or all the other issues that are not from God, we have a God given right to refuse entry of things into our bodies, and minds. We can cancel the assignment of these things by the power of the blood of Jesus Christ and His name.

INHERITANCE

So, what did we inherit from Jesus

Romans 12:1-2 I beseech you therefore, brethren, by the mercies of God, that you present your bodies a living sacrifice, holy acceptable unto God, which is your reasonable service. 2. And be not conformed to this world: but be ye transformed by the renewing of your mind, that ye may prove what is that good, and acceptable and perfect will of God.

1 John 4:4 You are of God, little children, and have overcome them, because greater is He that is in you, than he that is in the world. 5. They are of the world: therefore speak they of the world, and the world hears them, 6. We are of God: he that knows God hears us; he that is not of God hears not us, Hereby we know we the spirit of truth, and the spirit of error.

2 Corinthians 1:20 For all the promises of God in Him are yes and Amen, unto the glory of God by us.

We have a right to step on cancer and say you cannot come in. Christians allow things to come on them.

OVERCOMERS

Jesus said we are overcomers in this life.

1 John 4.4 You are of God little children, and have overcome them; because greater is He who is in you, than he who is in the world

.

1 John 5.5 Who is the he that overcomes the world, but he that believes that Jesus Christ is the Son of God?

You are what you see	Psalms 101:3
You are what you speak	Proverbs 18:21
You are what you read	Deuteronomy 17:19
	Joshua 8:34
You are what you think	Matthew 12:24
	Philippians 4:8
You are what you eat	Genesis 2:16

SEE - *Psalms 101:3 I will set no wicked thing before mine eyes:*

SPEAK - *Proverbs 18:21 Death and life are in the power of the tongue, and they that love it shall eat the fruit thereof.*

READ - *Deuteronomy 17:19 And it shall be with him, and he shall read therein all the days of his life: that he may learn to fear the Lord his God, to keep all the words of this law and these statutes, to do them.*

Joshua 8:34 And afterwards he read all the words of the law, the blessings and the cursing's, according to all that is written in the book of the law.

THINK - *Matthew 12:34 Out of the abundance of the heart the mouth speaks.*

Philippians 4:8 Finally, brethren, whatsoever things are true, whatsoever things are honest, whatsoever things are just, whatsoever things are pure, whatsoever things are lovely, whatsoever things are of good report; if there be any virtue, and if there be any praise think on these things.

EAT - *Genesis 2:16 And the Lord God commanded the man, saying of every tree of the garden thou mayest freely eat.*

GOD EXPECTS US TO DO RIGHT BY OUR BODIES

Eating Right, Exercising and getting enough Rest.

We all live in a house made of some form of wood, siding, brick or concrete. We can take care of the house keep it clean, keep the yard looking decent, or we can let it get filthy on the inside and have a trashy yard on the outside. We have a choice. We can either let it go to ruins or make it look great.

We live in a flesh covered house called the body and God expects us to do our part in staying active and eating healthier foods. We can't expect to stand in front of an oncoming train and say oh please Lord don't let it hit me when He has given us legs to walk off the track. We cannot continually be a couch potato eating and drinking junk food and expect this body to be healthy. We cause a lot of problems ourselves then expect God to undo our mess. The mess we made. What goes in must come out. Junk in, junk out; word of God in, word of God will come out

I found this out the hard way recently while babysitting my grandbaby. I did not eat healthy like I know I am supposed to, instead I junked out on candy, chocolate and snacks every day and didn't eat regular meals for a couple of months. (guess what?) I got sick and who's fault was that? mine of course. Junk in junk out. I did not take care of this temple. First time I had been sick in many, many years. I got so busy with grandbaby and let my guard down. And yes, it took me by surprise. I asked God what happened, then He let me know I had not taken care of myself. I didn't practice what I preached. So yes, eat healthy and take care of yourself.

All the fillers they put in food.
Are filling out our bodies.
Humm, that sounds like truth to me.

Read the food labels, there is so much artificial stuff and preservatives put into the food we eat. For example, to make pancakes you need flour, eggs, and milk. That is pretty much it, 3 ingredients. But you look at a box of pancake mix and you will see approximately 20 ingredients. I know they have to put things in there to make the product have a longer shelf life and I know we cannot avoid these foods sometimes, but we can balance it with the intake of good organic and/or real natural food products. Some brands of foods have less bad ingredients than others so look at the labels. Even our soaps, shampoos and toothpastes have some really bad, toxic and crazy stuff added to them.

The food industry has realized the public wants healthier choices so in most food stores now you see a lot of Organic food, Whole grains, Non-GMO, no artificial sugars, colours, sweeteners, or flavors, no preservatives, no MSG

My goodness what have we been putting in our bodies all these years if they are now taking them out because they are bad for us.   Humm!

A family member was taking prescribed drugs for years for an ailment but has now discovered it has damaged his kidneys and weakened other parts of his body. He now has to walk around with portable oxygen. Seven years ago, my son had lost weight about 20lbs without trying. He went to the doctor to see what would help him gain it back, the doctor told him he was depressed and prescribed him antidepressants, just one of the many side effects was thoughts of suicide. Wow just wow! A friend that worked at a drug store said if you start on that medication it is very hard to get off because the body won't let you. My son and I did our own research and it had nothing to do with gaining weight which is what he wanted to do, so of course he didn't take it and besides that he wasn't depressed anyway so it should never have been prescribed for him.

We are bombarded by so many commercials for food and drugs that possibly are not good for our health. It is our responsibility to be cognizant of all that we put into our bodies and our family's bodies. I am not saying don't take medication prescribed for you, just make sure you do research on it.

Americans spend more out of pocket per year than any other western nation on prescription drugs but are not any healthier. In fact the people in the USA are one of the unhealthiest people in the world. Something is wrong with that picture. Just research that and see for yourself.

Quite often the drugs approved by the FDA are recalled. Why- follow the money. God expects us to use wisdom and do what is right for our health. Several years ago I heard someone say;

If God made it eat it, if man made it do not eat much of it. I have tried to follow that most of my life, because it makes sense, God has provided everything we need to live.

David Van Koevering, a Christian Quantum Physicist says, **"what the cells are fed today they become tomorrow."** So if you give your body unhealthy food today, the cells can't rebuild as normal cells and can become rouge then you can have cells turning into diseased cells. He has some great CD's and DVD's

The body has to be subject to our spiritual house in order for things to work for us in the natural house, meaning the body. Our spirit man must be fed with the word, worship and prayer in order to stay strong. That's when the spirit man tells the body you're not lined up with the word of God. Do we really believe what God says or is it only surface belief? The devil will always try to give you doubts about Gods word and what it says to you.

> *Genesis 3:1 Now the serpent was more subtle than any animal of the field which Yahweh God had made. He said to the woman, "**Has God really said, You shall not eat of any tree of the garden.**** Emphasis added

WE CANNOT PICK AND CHOOSE WHICH PARTS OF GOD'S WORD WE WANT TO BELIEVE

I have a right not to be sick according to God's word. If we have a right to refuse sickness why accept sickness.

Abraham did not look at the earthly circumstances,

> *Romans 4:19-21 And being not weak in faith, he considered not his own body now dead, when he was about an hundred years old, neither yet the deadness of Sarah's womb, 20. He staggered not at the promise*

of God through unbelief: but was strong in faith, giving glory to God: 21. And being fully persuaded that, what he had promised, he was able also to perform.

God said it and Abraham believed it. Abraham believed through faith in what God said to him. **What about You!**

Faith is believing.
Believing is trust.
Trust is knowing.
Knowing is knowledge.

Knowledge is the fact of knowing someone by an intimate connection and/or experience. You either believe God's word or you don't.

An interesting side note here;

*Proverbs 3:5-8 Trust in the Lord with all thine heart; and lean not unto thine own understanding. 6. In all thy ways **acknowledge** Him, and He shall direct thy path. 7. Be not wise in thine own eyes: fear the Lord and depart from evil. 8. It shall be health to thy navel, and marrow to thy bones. Emphasis added.*

When we talk about acknowledging something we are accepting something; like accepting that there is a God. We acknowledge that the sun is always shining even when we can't see it. But The word acknowledge in the Strong's Concordance H3045 means to KNOW Him intimately. when we know Him and have a deep relationship with Him, He will direct our paths, so it would read:

> **Proverbs 3:6: In all your ways <u>know</u> Him intimately and He will direct your path.**

> *Proverbs 3:8 tells that it is health to our navel, and marrow to our bones.*

The word navel in Strong's Concordance H8270, figuratively speaking says, the navel is considered the center of strength also the word marrow H8250 is refreshment to our bones.

Faith is seeing what God sees, God sees life, wholeness, peace, joy, happiness. He does not despair, sickness, misery, tears, pain.

> *Hebrews 11:1 Now faith is the substance of things hoped for, the evidence of things not seen.*

John 6:63 It is the spirit that quickens: the flesh profits nothing, but the words that I speak to you they are spirit and they are life.

Words are impactful. From the beginning in Genesis God spoke everything into existence with words, creative words. Jesus became the living Word of God incarnate, the embodiment of God Himself.

Do you know who you are in Christ?
Do you know what you have in Christ?
Do you know what Christ has given you?
Do you know what you are to do with what you have in Christ? Questions Questions.

There are plenty of books on how to gain Godly wisdom, how to be debt free, how to get saved, but what about disease and sickness free.

How can we unequivocally say God heals, when were not sure if He will or will not, that doesn't make any sense at all. We cannot go in and pray for someone's healing and hope for the best or have a win some lose some ideology. God is consistent and constant; the same yesterday, today and forever. **He didn't move from us; we moved away from Him. He didn't change His mind; we changed ours**

from the truth. He changes not and He is not a respecter of persons.

> *Malachi 3:6 For I am the Lord, I change not.*

> *Hebrews 13:8 Jesus Christ the same yesterday, and today, and forever.*

> *Acts 10:34 Then Peter opened his mouth and said of a truth I perceive that God is not respecter of persons.*

People accept sickness before they accept God's healing or His word on healing. They believe Jesus and the disciples had power from God to heal, but today they do not.

If we believe God can heal us after we are sick, why can't we believe God can stop sickness before it starts. **Just a thought.**

When did people stop believing and start doubting?

We have become filled with the knowledge of the world instead of the knowledge of God. We have moved away from God and our reliance and need of Him it's because of our own intellectual knowledge due to the technology available to us now, because of this many think they have no need of God. If they even believe there is a God.

Jesus came to bring us the kingdom of heaven, which is everything that is good in heaven, health, peace, joy, happiness, prosperity, love and much more.

LIFE IS THE WORD OF GOD
GOD IS LIFE

Hebrews 4:12 For the word of God is living and active, and sharper than any two-edged sword, piercing even to the dividing of soul and spirit, of both joints and marrow, and quick to discern the thoughts and intents of the heart.

The word of God is living, active and sharper than any two-edged sword, a two-edged sword is razor sharp on both sides of the blade and can slice both going up and going down. The word of God is living, as in alive like you are reading this, and active like a little child. Then why do we have a hard time believing and trusting in it.

The word of God is a living word. So, if its living that means when we speak it leaves our mouths alive and goes into the natural and spiritual world. For example, we can understand when someone has the flu and they are coughing, sneezing. We cannot see the germs, but we know the germs are leaving their mouth alive and going into the air and we do not want to breath in their germs. So how much more powerful and alive the word of God is when spoken into the atmosphere both spiritual and natural.

Numbers 20:8 Moses was told to SPEAK to the rock to get water out.

Remember:

Proverbs 18:21 Death and life are in the power of the tongue; And they that love it shall eat the fruit therof.

We are to speak life so we can have the fruit of life.

It doesn't say do life, it says SPEAK LIFE.

Psalms 103:20 Bless the Lord, you His angels, that excel in strength, that do His commandments, hearkening unto the voice of the Lord.

The Darby translation
*Psalms 103:20 Bless Jehovah, ye his angels, mighty In strength, that **execute** His word, hearkening unto the voice of His word.* Emphasis added

Youngs Literal Translation
*Psalms 103:20 Bless Jehovah, ye His messengers, **mighty in power**—doing His word, To hearken to the voice of His word.* Emphasis added

World English Bible (WEB)
*Psalms 103:20 Praise Yahweh, you angels of His, who are mighty in strength, who **fulfill** His word.*
Emphasis added

The angels of God hear His word being spoken by us and when they hear the word, they become mighty and excel in strength. they go do what was spoken. It is God's word and the moment they hear His word they rush to go do it, as in healing, deliverance, salvation, and miracles. All we have done is spoken God's word out loud, but it lives and goes forth into the spiritual realm.

Isaiah 55:11 So shall my word be that goes forth out of my mouth: it shall not return unto me void, but it shall accomplish that which I please, and it shall prosper in the thing where to I sent it.

Psalms 107: 20 He sent His word and healed them and delivered them from all their destruction.

God said He sends forth His word and it does not come back void (unaccomplished) but accomplishes what it was sent to do.

Matthew 21:18-22 Now in the morning as he returned into the city, he hungered. 19. And when he saw a fig tree in the way, he came to it, and found nothing thereon, but leaves only, and said unto it, Let no fruit grow on thee henceforward forever. And presently the fig tree withered away. 20. And when the disciples saw it, they marveled, saying, How soon is the fig tree withered away!

21. Jesus answered and said unto them, Verily I say unto you, If ye have faith, and doubt not, ye shall not only do this which is done to the fig tree, but also if ye shall say unto this mountain, Be thou removed, and be thou cast into the sea; it shall be done. 22. And all things, whatsoever ye shall ask in prayer, believing, ye shall receive.

OUR WORDS ARE EITHER LIFE GIVING OR LIFE DESTROYING

In the natural you can put down a child all his life by telling him he's dumb, stupid, he can't learn anything, and he will grow up believing he is dumb, stupid and good for nothing. The spoken word is powerful much more than we realize.

Proverbs 6.2 Thou art snared by the words of your mouth; you are taken with the words of your mouth.

We must have God's word in us for God's word to come out.

The later part of;

> *Matthew 12: 34 for out of the abundance*
> *of the heart (soul) the mouth speaks.*

Whatever your heart is full of will come out. We must speak LIFE always.

So, in Psalms 103: 20   The the angels can take the word of God we speak, excel in strength and go do His word.

Do we not think the evil spirits can do the same with our negative words?

Radio waves go through the air; but do we see or hear them? NO, but we know they are there, listening to your radio, watching TV, or talking on your cell phone, you do not see cords hanging from the sky to your cell phone. Its invisible electromagnetic waves passing right in front of you and right through you, but you do not see or feel anything.

Our words are floating around in the atmosphere of the natural world and the spirit world. Either the angels of God or the demon spirits will take those words we have spoken and use them for us or against us. For example, how many times do you hear someone say, "I think I'm coming down with the flu" or "I have cancer, I have diabetes, I have heart problems" etc etc etc. Others will say "MY arthritis, MY cancer, My diabetes, MY heart disease" they are claiming ownership of it by saying it's MINE.

I say, My children, or My grandchildren because they belong to me they are mine. I am claiming ownership of them because they belong to ME.

I see demon spirits just waiting to give you the symptoms of what you just said and if you say it long enough you will bring it to fruition.

Job 3:25 For the thing which I greatly feared is come upon me, and that which I was afraid of is come unto me.

Whoa that's powerful and certainly an eye opener for all of us. As we think so shall we be. Again a mindset. What is your mind set on?

We need to say, I am healed, and the manifestation of my healing is on its way according to God's word and My God cannot lie!

We can speak the same thing for deliverance, prosperity, peace, joy, our families' salvation, and whatever need we have. We must speak **LIFE.**

> *Titus 1:2 In hope of eternal life, which God, that cannot lie, promised before the world began.*

> *Philippians 4:19 But my God shall supply all our need according to His riches in glory by Christ Jesus.*

Our words come from the seat of our emotions, so whatever has been put in there will come out for good or bad. That's why it's imperative for us to put God's word into our being daily.
We must have God's word in us for God's word to come out,

> *Luke 6:4 A good man out of the good treasure of his heart brings forth that which is good; and evil man out of treasure of his heart brings for that which is evil: for out of the abundance of the heart his mouth speaks.*

In other words, whatever your heart is full of will come out.

True examples; one time a person was on the phone with a family member, when suddenly they ran into the back of a truck and it killed them, the last word that was heard was sh--. What was in their heart, very sad.

Next there were 3 ladies in a car all supposed to be Christians, when suddenly they were about to run into something. Two of the ladies started praying and the other lady started screaming obscenities. What was in her heart?

Effective way to tell what may be in your heart is when you are startled, or something suddenly happens what are the first words out of your mouth? Pay attention to what you speak in that moment.

Another time a couple and their young grandson were heading home from vacation when an 18-wheel truck pulled over on them hitting them in the side of a very small car spinning them around. They ended up in front of the truck as it traveled and pushed them down the interstate at 65 miles an hour. The woman in the car was heard to be saying Jesus, Jesus, Jesus as they were being pushed sideways down the road. MIRACULOUSLY they lived and walked away.

What is in **your** heart.

*James 3:6 And the tongue is a fire, a
world of iniquity: so is the tongue
among our members, that it defiles the
whole body, and sets on fire the course
of nature; and it is set on fire by hell.*

NEW CREATURE

*Romans 12:2 And be not conformed to
this world, but be transformed by the
renewing of you mind, so that you may
prove what is that good, and acceptable,
and perfect will of God.*

Renew means to make new again. Renew your
mind with the word of God daily. The devil comes
to steal our word because he knows the word of
God the living word builds your faith, which
strengthens you and strengthens your soul.

*2 Corinthians 5:17 Therefore if any man
be in Christ, he is a new creature: old
things are passed away; behold all
things are become new.*

We have been made a new creature, Strong's number G2537 and Thayer's Greek lexicon, the meaning is, recently made, fresh, new, superior to what it succeeds, a newer model of the old, a newer a version of the old. So when we accept Jesus as our personal savior we become a brand new person inside and out. **WOW!!!**

Philippians 4:13 I can do all things through Christ which strengthens me.

The word is also life to your spirit to bring you, to a new level in Him, and it inspires you from the inside out.

1 John 4:4 Greater is He, that is in you, than he that is in the world.

Who do you think is in you?
<u>The Holy spirit is in you.</u>

Ephesians 4:23 And that you be renewed the spirit in of your mind.

I believe when we speak God's word, sing psalms, worship, and love Him it puts a hedge of protection around us so the oppressive spirits have to leave. When we speak in tongues we speak mysteries in the spirit world, and we renew our own spirit. When you quote God's word out loud to yourself you send demons running, they don't like you knowing God's word because they know it empowers you

> *Isaiah 53:4 Surely, He has borne our GRIEFS, and carried our SORROWS: yet we did esteem Him stricken, smitten of God, and AFFLICTED. Emphasis added*

He carried our sicknesses and pain, both physical and mental, we didn't give it a second thought or value what He did. He was injured, beaten, and wounded. That's just verse 4.

> *Isaiah 53: 5. But He was WOUNDED for our TRANSGRESSIONS, He was BRUISED for our INIQUITIES: the CHASTISEMENT of our PEACE was upon Him; and with His STRIPES we are HEALED. Emphasis added*

Verse 5, meanings from Strong's concordance

Wounded = defiled, profane, pollute, pierce.
Transgressions = sin, transgress, rebellion.

Bruised = to beat, to crush, beat to pieces.
Iniquities = punishment for our sin.
Chastisement = discipline, correction.
PEACE =, safety, welfare, great (good) health, prosperity, peace and contentment, favor, happy, wellbeing.
Stripes = wound, blow, bruise with black and blue marks on skin.
Healed = to heal, to make healthy, repair, make whole people and nations.

We should have been rebuked chastised, disciplined, and given correction. but instead Jesus took all of that on Himself for all mankind and gave us His peace. In that 5-letter word PEACE from Strong's Concordance H7965 He gave us peace that passes all understanding, safety, a feeling of wellbeing, prosperity, wholeness, favor, rest, peace, and health.

HOW GREAT IS OUR GOD

Isaiah 53, We ARE healed, whole, delivered, set free, and forgiven, all our needs are met right in this one verse. We don't live in the real world where God is. This life is but a vapor according to James 4:14, here for a short while then gone.

We've got to know that we are made of spirit soul and body. Mark, a dear friend, once said "whatever you feed the most will live and overcome the others and be in charge, it will rule and reign". The word of God is more alive than you are. When the body dies it will decay and go back to the dust of the earth.

Hebrews 4:12 For that the word of God quick, and powerful, and sharper than any two-edged sword piercing even to the dividing asunder of soul and spirit, and of the joins and the marrow, and is a discerner of the thoughts and intents of the heart.

The soul is the mind, will, and emotion, and the spirit is from God. Which do you feed? Even in the natural words are alive. If you cry for help someone will hear and respond. The word "help" is carried through the atmosphere to their ears, so our words carry on through the spirit world.

In Matthew 12:36-37 But I say unto you, That every idle word that men shall speak they shall give account thereof in the day of judgment. 37.For by thy words thou shalt be justified, and by thy words shall be condemned.

So we are told we will be judged for every idle word we speak, if we do not repent for it. God hears ALL our words, all the time. We must eat the word of God and digest it, so we can speak it. In the normal process, of eating food, the nutrients are sent through the body and the rest is eliminated. When we eat the word of God it will come forth out of our mouth. If we eat enough of it the soulish man will line up with the spirit man, then the body will line up beside them to create; **One solid God infused powerhouse.**

We are dysfunctional beings when we do not line up with God's word; but instead our spirit lives for God, our soul goes in his corner with fears, anxieties, and the body feels sickly because they are all fragmented from God. The bible says a house divided cannot stand Matthew 12:25 and Mark 3:25.

We must be proactive, or we will not live a victorious life as God intended. God has made a provision for everything we need, but we have neglected to take hold.

Psalms 68:19 Blessed be the Lord who daily loads us with benefits.

If your dad was a very wealthy man and you knew he would give you anything you needed. Say you had a great need, but instead of asking your dad to help you, you went around wringing your hands saying, what will I do? how can I get help? that would be very silly on our part, but that is what we do with our heavenly Father.
He has provided for everything we will ever need.

WAR

People don't understand we are in a spiritual war in this world, Christians and non-Christians. If we are in a war then we have to fight in the spirit as Paul tells.

> *Ephesians 6:11 Finally, be strong in the Lord, and in the strength of his might. 11. Put on the whole armor of God, that you may be able to stand against the wiles of the devil. 12. For our wrestling is not against flesh and blood, but against the principalities, against the powers, against the world's rulers of the darkness of this age, and against the spiritual forces of wickedness in the heavenly places. 13. Therefore put on the whole armor of God, that you may*

be able to withstand in the evil day, and having done all, to stand. 14. Stand therefore, having the utility belt of truth buckled around your waist, and having put on the breastplate of righteousness, 15. and having fitted your feet with the preparation of the Good News of peace, 16. above all, taking up the shield of faith, with which you will be able to quench all the fiery darts of the evil one. 17. And take the helmet of salvation, and the sword of the Spirit, spoken word" of God;.

War not against flesh and blood, but in the Spirit;

This is the mentality we must have;

"devil back off and back out because we

WILL"

Fight for our kids
Fight for our families
Fight for our marriages
Fight for our jobs
Fight for our finances
Fight for our health

*1 Timothy 6:12 Fight the good fight of
faith, lay hold on eternal life, whereunto
you are called, and has professed a good
profession before many witnesses.*

*2 Corinthians 2:16 "For who has known
the mind of the Lord, that he may instruct
him? But we have the mind of Christ.*

God is structured, God is organized. Nothing is
happenstance with God; it's orchestrated. Why
would we go through life as a Christian not
knowing from one day to the next if we were going
to get very sick or have a terrible accident.

We are the army of God, like an earthly army
they are taught, trained, disciplined. Their whole
demeanor changes, they become more self-
controlled, respectful. They are trained as one
unit, and like mindedness. They learn to march in
order with others, synchronized with the group
marching lowering weapons, and standing to
attention. In essence the military brakes you then
remolds you into what they want. Their whole
mode of thinking changes and they become
disciplined and full of self-control.

So, it is in the army of God. He wants our thinking to change so we think like He does. What God thinks we think. It maybe irrational to the world or even to ourselves as to how we used to think. But we now think like Christ because we have the mind of Christ we don't do what we used to do or say what we used to say or think like we used to think. We have been trained by God and His word, we are more disciplined, now we instantly start to think like Christ and do what Christ would. We don't think like the world does anymore and we do not accept the negative things the world wants to offer us. We've been trained to think and act like the Father. Would He accept sickness? NO!!! We are not of this world anymore. Our homeland is heaven.

That's how we win a war in the Spirit

If you believe in your heart you will have whatever you ask God for.

Matt 21:22 And ALL things, whatsoever you shall ask in prayer, believing, you shall receive.

Mark 11:23-24 For verily I say unto you, That whosoever shall say unto this

mountain, Be thou removed, and be thou
cast into the sea, and shall not doubt in
his heart, but shall believe that those
things which he saith shall come to pass;
he shall have whatsoever he saith.

Everything God did He spoke it into existence. Everything that exists has a vibration and frequency, everything. Again, David Van Koevering has some excellent teaching on this, you can find them on you tube at **David@elsewhen.com.**

In 2 Chronicles 20, Jehoshaphat was told that the children of Moab, Ammon and others were coming to overtake them. The people began to fear so Jehoshaphat set himself to seek the Lord. He reminds God that they built a sanctuary for His name, saying in;

2 Chronicles 20:9 If, when evil cometh
upon us, as the sword, judgement, or
pestilence, or famine, we stand before this
house, and in thy presence, (for thy name
is in this house,) and cry unto thee in our
affliction, then thou will hear and help.

Are we not the temple of God **NOW?** We are His house and He resides in us.

1 Corinthians 3:16 Know ye not that ye are the temple of God, and that the Spirit of God dwells in you?

Jehoshaphat went to the temple where God was dwelling to get help, but we are the house that now holds the presence of God. God and His word now dwells in us. We are His temple, so we have His power and authority to use His word to come against sickness and disease and refuse it entry into our temple.

Father God I plead the blood and apply the blood of Jesus Christ over my family (list names) friends, Israel and nations to protect from all sickness, harm and danger, accidents and incidents of all kinds, and against all wickedness that would come against us in Jesus mighty powerful name. Thank You Jesus.

Isaiah 49:16 Behold, I have graven you on the palms of my hands; thy walls are continually before me.

Meaning of Walls in Strong's Concordance H2346
"Is a wall of protection"

He has each one of us named in the palm of
His hands and has a ***wall of protection*** around us.
God is forever with us and on our side.
What an awesome promise that our Heavenly
Father watches over us day and night 24/7.
Thank Your Lord.

Jesus has done all He can do for our healing and wellbeing; the rest is up to us.

ALL WE HAVE TO DO IS

BELIEVE

WILL YOU BELIEVE

WILL   YOU

BELIEVE

.

www.ingramcontent.com/pod-product-compliance
Lightning Source LLC
Chambersburg PA
CBHW020950030426
42339CB00004B/35